QUILT
SAVVY

ONE-PATCH
SCRAP QUILTS
PAT YAMIN

American Quilter's Society
P. O. Box 3290 • Paducah, KY 42002-3290
www.AmericanQuilter.com

Located in Paducah, Kentucky, the American Quilter's Society (AQS) is dedicated to promoting the accomplishments of today's quilters. Through its publications and events, AQS strives to honor today's quiltmakers and their work and to inspire future creativity and innovation in quiltmaking.

EDITOR: HELEN SQUIRE
GRAPHIC DESIGN: ELAINE WILSON & MARY BETH HEAD
COVER DESIGN: MICHAEL BUCKINGHAM
HOW-TO AND QUILT PHOTOGRAPHY: CHARLES R. LYNCH

Library of Congress Cataloging-in-Publication Data

Yamin, Pat.
   Quilt savvy:one-patch scrap quilts / by Pat Yamin.
      p. cm.
   Summary: "Using one or two shapes, make a modern version of a classic quilt from the three dozen patterns provided. Patterns are arranged by degree of sewing difficulty and include a number of patterns from the Kansas City Star series. Includes quilting history and memorabilia"--Provided by the publisher.
      ISBN 978-1-57432-937-7
      1. Patchwork--Patterns. 2. Quilting--Patterns. I. Title.

TT835.Y375 2007
746.46'041--dc22
                        200723186

Additional copies of this book may be ordered from the American Quilter's Society, PO Box 3290, Paducah, KY 42002-3290, toll free 800-626-5420, or online at www.americanquilter.com.

Proudly printed and bound in the United States of America

COVER: **ELONGATED HEXAGON,** 68" x 84", antique top, quilted by Laura Lipski. Special thanks to Pier 1 Imports, Paducah, Kentucky, for location photography. COLLECTION OF THE AUTHOR.

RIGHT: **HOUSES (DETAIL),** 37" x 36", made by Peggy Weichel, Mt. Plymouth, Florida

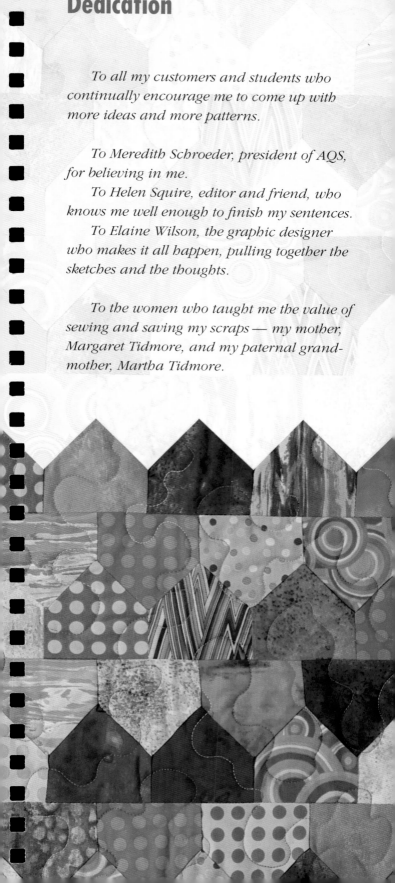

Dedication

To all my customers and students who continually encourage me to come up with more ideas and more patterns.

To Meredith Schroeder, president of AQS, for believing in me.

To Helen Squire, editor and friend, who knows me well enough to finish my sentences.

To Elaine Wilson, the graphic designer who makes it all happen, pulling together the sketches and the thoughts.

To the women who taught me the value of sewing and saving my scraps — my mother, Margaret Tidmore, and my paternal grand-mother, Martha Tidmore.

Acknowledgments

I wish to thank all of my friends, family, and quilting colleagues for helping me move the idea of scraps out of the closet and into a book.

I would like to give a very special thank you to the following quilters: Stevii Graves, Lynne Williams, Kimberley Graf, Angie Stevenson, Vicki Shephard, Margaret Phillips, Tammie Griswold, Suzanne Rudisill, Vicki Romaine Cohn, and Rhona Hiney— as well as to those quilters whose work appears in the book.

Contents

Introduction

L iving in a home built in the 1890s has inspired me with admiration and curiosity for antiques, whether they be quilts, china, or the original wallpaper that is still on our attic walls. The stairs creak and remind me that this home is more than a century old. Perhaps the house has instilled in me a quest to learn more about the past. An interest in vintage items (especially textiles) created the desire to seek out old quilts, blocks, and tops. In turn, I became an antique "junkie," addicted to rescuing those that were tossed into cardboard boxes or musty trunks and destined to be cut apart and made into stuffed animals, chic vests, etc. The collection soon narrowed down to One-Patch, scrap, or charm quilts. Friends shared my interest and we salvaged and traded the quilts we found.

Like Grandma's favorite Sunday perfume you never forgot, the old patterns brought back fond memories of sleeping under a handmade scrap quilt in her white metal four-poster featherbed. My sister and I lay awake at night counting the patches and running our fingers across Grandma's quilting stitches, so even and perfect.

As the familiar saying goes, "*What's old is new again.*" So in this book, I am sharing with you my collection of 36 patterns for One-Patch or scrap quilts from which you can make templates. Some are quite easy like the Tumbler and Brick patterns. Others are a bit more complicated such as the Quilter's Fan or Picket Fence. But there is a One-Patch pattern for everyone.

When you see my collection of historic tops, paper patterns, and clippings from the *Kansas City Star* newspaper, you will feel inspired to create them using today's fabrics and supplies. The quilting tools may be different but the patterns are the same great classics our grandmothers lovingly used.

I hope this book might encourage you to trade and exchange fabrics with other quilters, much like our grandmothers did many years ago. After all, patches of fabric record our lives and memorable times. A simple square quilt made for my mother and brothers had fabric from my father's shirts. Every time they sleep under it, memories return of him mowing the lawn, painting the side of the garage, and running out of barbecue charcoal at a family picnic — recollections to share with later generations.

If you discover a One-Patch pattern not illustrated and identified in this book, I hope you will share it with me!

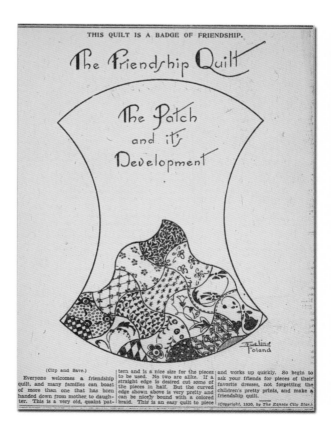

THIS QUILT IS A BADGE OF FRIENDSHIP.

The Friendship Quilt

The Patch and its Development

Eveline Foland

(Clip and Save.)

Everyone welcomes a friendship quilt, and many families can boast of more than one that has been handed down from mother to daughter. This is a very old, quaint pattern and is a nice size for the pieces to be used. No two are alike. If a straight edge is desired cut some of the pieces in half. But the curved edge shown above is very pretty and can be nicely bound with a colored braid. This is an easy quilt to piece and works up quickly. So begin to ask your friends for pieces of their favorite dresses, not forgetting the children's pretty prints, and make a friendship quilt.

(Copyright, 1930, by The Kansas City Star.)

Historical Retrospect

I n the latter part of the nineteenth century, mothers were busy with homemaking and raising families. They delighted in free time spent socializing. Sometimes it was a quilting bee or a fundraiser for their church, and children accompanied mothers, keeping busy jumping rope, playing ball, or shooting marbles.

Perhaps it was while the mothers were occupied with sewing that the children began trading and collecting buttons among themselves. In the late 1850s, as their collections grew, the buttons were strung onto heavy cords and called "button strings" or "memory strings." Button collections were quite prized, and the gift of a button was believed to bring good fortune to the recipient. A common superstition held that if a girl had 999 buttons on her string, the gentleman who provided the 1000th button would become her future husband.

Collecting is an age-old American pastime. Our grandmothers collected and traded fabric and recipes, farmers traded planting information and stories, children traded books and marbles — much as we collect quilting patterns or Featherweight sewing machines today.

The young women of the era traded and exchanged fabric, each piece holding a special memory of who or where it came from. Gathering the fabric and making sure no two patches were the same was a quest in a class of its own. Consequently, because of the scarcity of different fabrics available, few charm quilts were made or remain intact from this era.

Perhaps the idea of scrap quilts arose from this same need—using fabric from Julie's dress, Sam's shirt, or Grandma's apron to make a quilt. And so the "beggar's quilt" idea was born because you begged or traded enough fabric to complete your quilt.

In January 1835, *Godey's Lady's Book* published the first quilt pattern in the shape of a hexagon. The hexagon continues to reign as the most popular One-Patch pattern because of its versatility in creating other designs, such as half hexagon, 60-degree diamond, and equilateral triangle, to name just a few. Many who never made another quilt succeeded in finishing a Grandmother's Flower Garden quilt!

One-Patch, Scrap, and Charm Quilts

A One-Patch pattern is a single shape (hexagon, diamond, square or rectangle) without sashing or borders between the pieces. In this book, you will find a variety of patterns from simple to complex that provide allover designs for the quilt. Some scrap quilt patterns are considered "tessellations" because the pieces interlock leaving no gaps in the design.

In charm quilts, no two pieces of fabric are the same. Sometimes it takes two or three generations to complete a true charm quilt. I have a hexagon top that was begun in the late 1800s and had hexagons added through the 1930s. When finished, this top will be given to a local historical society because it is a record of the women in my family who made the quilt top.

Pattern Selection

B efore selecting a pattern for your quilt, be sure to study all 36 design ideas in the book. When you study the patterns carefully, you will realize that several have straight lines, while others have gentle curves.

The patterns are designated as "easy," "medium," and "harder." They are broken down into a simple format to get you started. If you are an experienced quilter and enjoy working with curves, go ahead and try the CLAMSHELL, page 118, or QUILTER'S FAN, page 122.

By 1934, there were quilt patterns being published weekly in over 400 newspapers in this country, the most popular being the *Kansas City Star*. Some of the patterns included in the book are from my own private collection. They had been traced onto church bulletins, cereal boxes, and pieces of cardboard and scrap paper. Most are a single shape but some are made of two pattern pieces. Women hoped to create more organized scrap quilts and so coordinated the fabrics with either white or muslin material to showcase designs (see OZARK COBBLESTONE, pages 134–137, in the bonus section.).

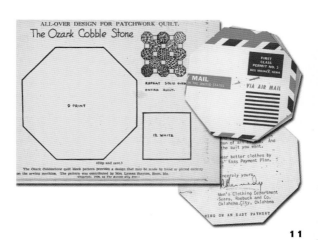

The Hunt for Fabrics

T hroughout history, quilters have been very generous sharing their time and fabrics. In October, 1905, Mrs. C. E. Anderson of Rolling Prairie, Indiana, wrote to the "Contributors' Gossip" column in *Hearth and Home*: "I shall be pleased to receive squares of gingham and calico, 4x4 inches, no two alike, for my charm quilt. Will return all favors."

You will find friends, guild members, and sewers willing to share their fabrics. Scraps packaged in plastic bags are popular and are readily available at quilt shops. Fat quarters in stores are attractively packaged and bound with ribbons, stuffed in canning jars, small baskets, miniature wooden crates, little pails, etc. Packets of color-coordinated fabric squares can also be purchased via mail order catalogs and online shopping Web sites. Yes, Grandma would definitely say we have come a long way! Online fabric exchanges have been set up on the Web as well.

Fabric tells a story of the history of clothing, home decorations, and quilting. Old fabrics and bags of scraps show up regularly at garage and tag sales. Look for boxes of linens, tablecloths, and pillowcases — sewing supplies and scraps are often hidden on the bottom and overlooked. To add to your stash of fabrics, you might ask your local fabric shop to save or sell you the salesmen's sample books of 3" or 4" squares at the end of their ordering season; then soak the individual squares in warm water to remove the glue. Once you decide to make a One-Patch or scrap quilt, the fun lies in collecting, sorting, and choosing your fabrics. Settle on a well-blended palette that has a

balance of lights and darks and includes an assortment of prints as well.

"How much piecing' a quilt is like livin' a life! You can give the same kind of pieces to two persons and one will make a 'nine-patch' and one'll make a 'wild goose chase' and there will be two quilts made out of the same kind of pieces, and jest as different as they can be. And that is jest the way with livin'. The Lord sends us the pieces, but we can cut them out and put 'em together pretty much to suit ourselves, and there's a heap more in the cuttin' out and the sewin' than there is in the caliker." [1]

1. Eliza Calvert Hall, *Aunt Jane of Kentucky* (Boston: Little Brown, and Company, 1909)

Preparing the Fabrics

There are many schools of thought on this subject. It is my preference to wash, dry, and iron all fabric before starting a project. You can toss it in the washing machine with a little detergent and the temperature setting on "warm." Prewashing shrinks the fabric slightly and removes sizing, making it easier to work with. If you are afraid a fabric will "bleed," discard it.

My suggestion for preparing large pieces of cotton is to cut it into one-yard pieces and "pink" or "scallop" the edges to prevent raveling during the washing and drying process. Before the fabric is completely dry, remove it from the dryer, spray with starch, and press. Then fold the fabric over a hanger that has a cardboard tube on the bottom.

Tip: Place cut fabric sections back on the same hanger as the one-yard pieces to avoid having to re-press. When laundering small pieces of fabric, place them in white nylon bags used for lingerie to prevent tangling.

Supplies

- ◆ Lots of scrap fabric:
  6 inch squares, fat eighths, or fat quarters

◆ Sewing machine	◆ Template plastic
◆ Thread	◆ ¼" or ⅛" hole punch
◆ Pins	◆ Sharpie® pen
◆ Fabric scissors	◆ Rotary cutter
◆ Ruler 6" x 12"	◆ Rotary mat
◆ Craft scissors	◆ Quilting needles

We are working with a lot of fabric that isn't necessarily yardage. Clear a space on your table or floor and gather all of your scraps, squares, and pieces. Scrap quilts are like a diary of your life. You have gathered fabric from family, friends, and exchanges, maybe even bought some on your own. As an analogy, the bright happy fabric represents the good times in your life, the medium colors when life seems to be going along smoothly, and the dark colors for life's disappointments. Just like our lives, quilts bring us joy and happiness. I hope you will sleep under your scrap quilt and have wonderful colorful dreams.

Making Your Templates

You have a choice of using different types of plastic to cut out your templates. It's entirely up you. Choose either plain white opaque or plastic sheets that have a ¼" grid. It's usually a good idea to trace the book pages and then use those to cut your patterns. The patterns can be pieced either by hand or by machine.

Machine Piecing

Trace the template using a Sharpie (a fine point marking pen with indelible ink).

Position the template plastic over the pattern piece and trace the pattern. The ¼" seam allowance has already been added.

Hand Piecing

Following the same method, trace the design and then use your ⅛" or ¼" hole punch to mark the ¼" at the corners for your seam allowance.

Resources

Accurate plastic templates — with slotted seam allowances added — are available from Come Quilt With Me (see Resources page 142). There are 36 shapes to choose from, each manufactured in the most popular sizes.

Tip: It is important that all of the pieces be cut out carefully. If they are not accurate, the pieces will not fit together correctly. It's usually a good idea to sew one unit together before cutting out all of your fabric pieces. I use sandpaper dots or InvisiGRIP™ from Omnigrid® on the back of the templates to prevent them from slipping while I am cutting.

Quilting

Hand Quilting

If you have been using vintage fabric for your One-Patch or scrap quilt, I highly recommend that you hand quilt it. Hand quilting is relaxing and very therapeutic in this fast-paced world we live in. You can sit with your family, take it with you in the car, and on your trips. You will be surprised how fast the quilting goes.

To begin quilting, cut a length of thread no longer than 18". Make a very small knot about ½" from the end of the thread. Take one or two small quilting stitches and give the thread a quick tug. This will pop the thread into the backing and batting. Continue to make short even running stitches through all of the layers. The stitches should be evenly spaced with the spaces between stitches about the same length as the stitches themselves.

To end the thread, take one very small backstitch. Push the point of the needle and thread through the backstitch and under the quilt top. Bring up your needle an inch away from where you made the backstitch. Carefully cut off the remaining thread.

Machine Quilting

Look carefully at the detailed close-ups of the 36 quilts featured. Various machine quilting designs have been used — swirls, meandering, diagonals, and vertical lines, as well as in-the-ditch stitches. Use your creativity! The blocks can be quilted one way and you can then change the design for the border. It's always a good idea if you're new to machine quilting to work on a practice piece first.

SQUARE, 46" x 46", made by Ann Fitzell, Yorktown Heights, New York. A great beginner's project creating Nine-Patch blocks and perfect to showcase your favorite color. The zigzag machine quilting separating each block adds interest to the finishing.

*E*EASY

Square

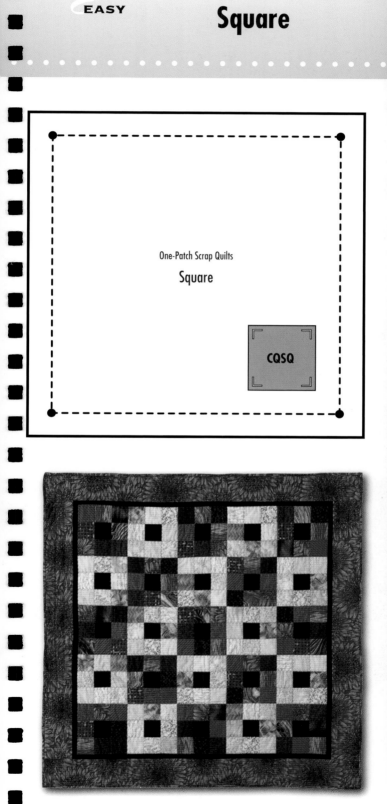

One-Patch Scrap Quilts

Square

CQSQ

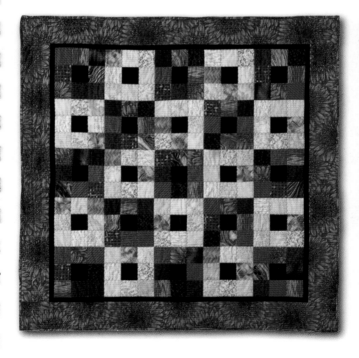

BRICK, author's collection. We see bricks in build-
ings and sidewalks every day when we are out walking.
It's the colors that add the inspiration to the piece.
These two blocks were made from shirting samples
from the 1800s.

*E*ASY

Brick

One-Patch Scrap Quilts
Brick

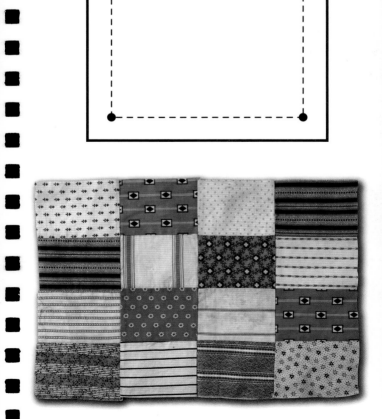

EQUILATERAL TRIANGLE, 46" x 43", made by Carolyn Barnett, Alta Loma, California. This template takes on a patriotic look by using red, white, and blue scraps arranged in a flag design. The meandering machine quilting adds texture to the design.

EASY

Equilateral Triangle

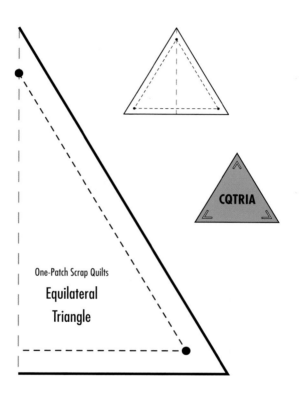

One-Patch Scrap Quilts
**Equilateral
Triangle**

CQTRIA

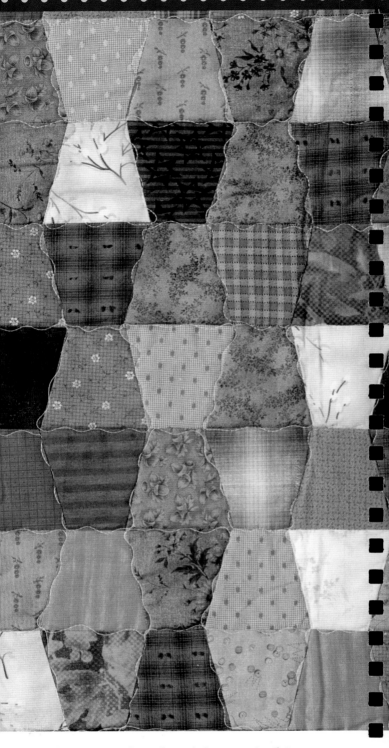

TUMBLER, 39" x 37", made by Janet Graff, San Diego, California. Purchasing a packet of Daiwabo fabric inspired me to choose the Tumbler shape for this quilt. Machine quilting with light thread outlining the shape lets the eye travel across the quilt. For a whimsical touch, the border was quilted in a meandering pattern.

EASY

Tumbler

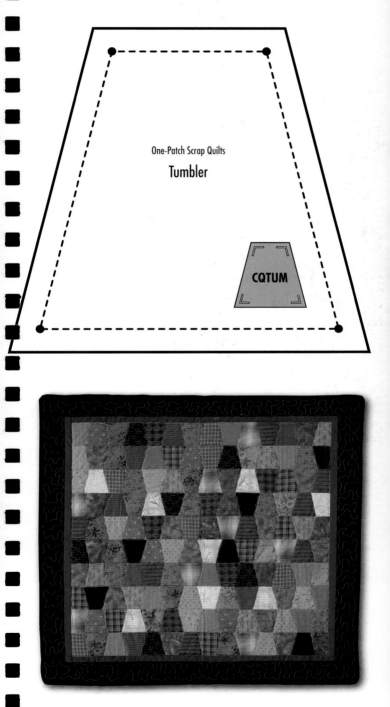

One-Patch Scrap Quilts

Tumbler

CQTUM

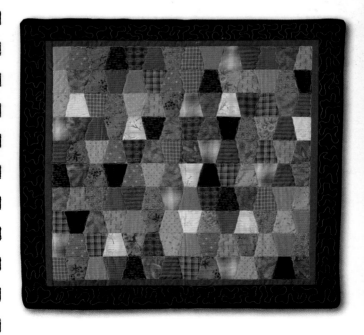

THIMBLE, 29" x 35", made by Carolyn Barnett, Alta Loma, California. What do you do with those tiny scraps we all end up with? Here's your answer! It is very simple to piece with all straight seams and it makes a great charm quilt.

ε EASY

Thimble

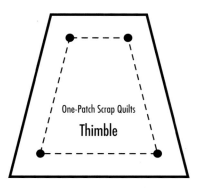

One-Patch Scrap Quilts

Thimble

CQTRIMIN'

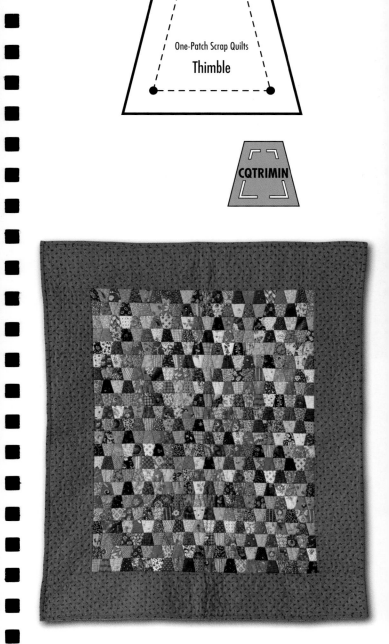

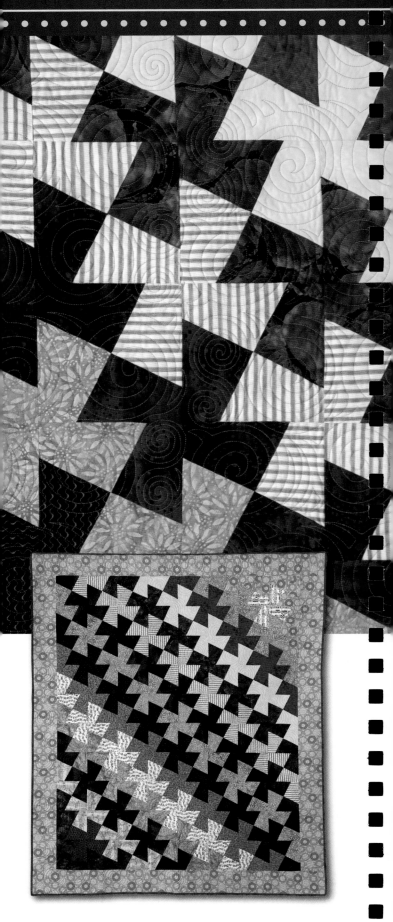

EASY Offset Square

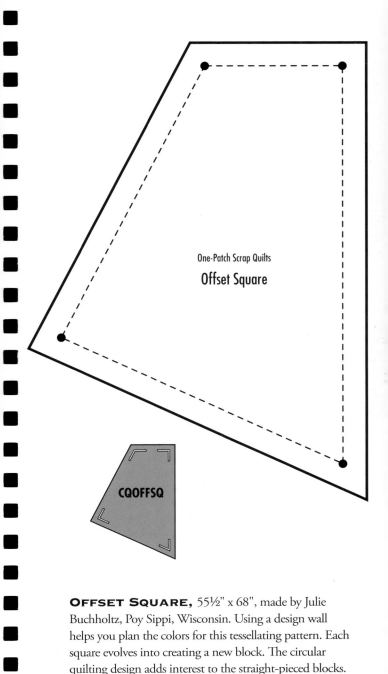

One-Patch Scrap Quilts

Offset Square

CQOFFSQ

OFFSET SQUARE, 55½" x 68", made by Julie
Buchholtz, Poy Sippi, Wisconsin. Using a design wall
helps you plan the colors for this tessellating pattern. Each
square evolves into creating a new block. The circular
quilting design adds interest to the straight-pieced blocks.

*E*ASY   **Half Rectangle**

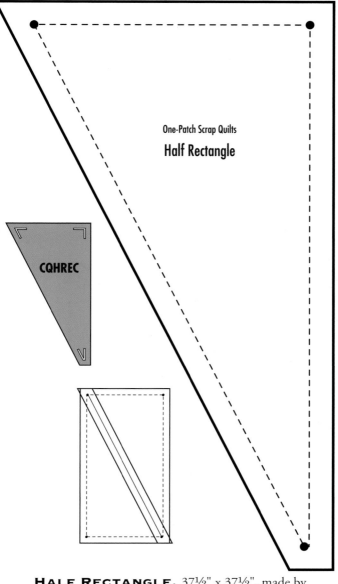

One-Patch Scrap Quilts
Half Rectangle

CQHREC

HALF RECTANGLE, 37½" x 37½", made by Linda Salitrynski, Rome, Pennsylvania. Four half-rectangle blocks come together to create a bold new design. Pastel batiks were used for the background allowing the darker design colors to pop. Quilting in the ditch provides structural support to the quilt.

Fun Patch

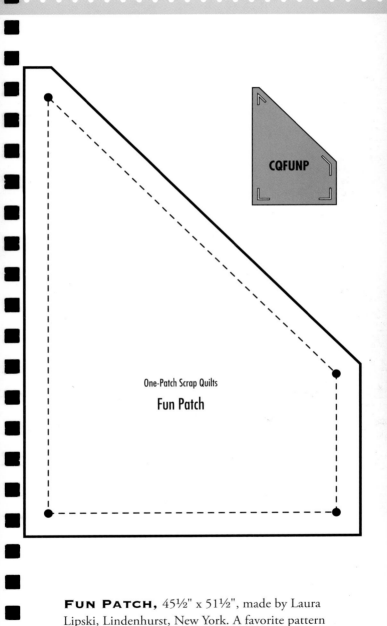

CQFUNP

One-Patch Scrap Quilts
Fun Patch

FUN PATCH, 45½" x 51½", made by Laura Lipski, Lindenhurst, New York. A favorite pattern for quilters, since you can play with light, medium, and dark fabric to come up with many variations of this one pattern piece. Look closely at the decorative stitching done between the seams. It adds interest as well as provides the necessary quilting.

*E*ASY   Windmill

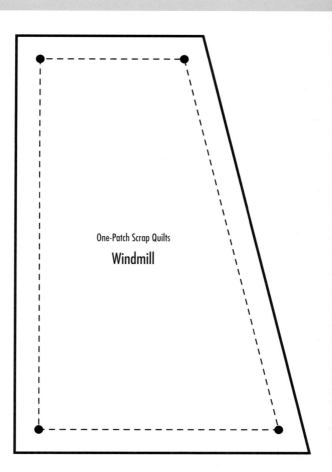

One-Patch Scrap Quilts
Windmill

CQWIND

WINDMILL, 39½" x 40½", made by Kathy D'Amour, Albertson, New York. A very popular and easy-to-sew quilt. Make it traditional or use some reproduction fabric. This soft palette of country prints works well to offset the pinwheels in shades of green. The machine quilting in a scroll design completes the look.

MINI-WINDMILL, 67" x 74", made by Carolyn Barnett, Alta Loma, California. The straight-line template and a bright background fabric were used to create a Four-Patch block. Multiple units can be made and repeated until there is enough for any size project. Edge-to-edge floral quilting unifies the design.

*ᴇ*EASY   **Mini-Windmill**

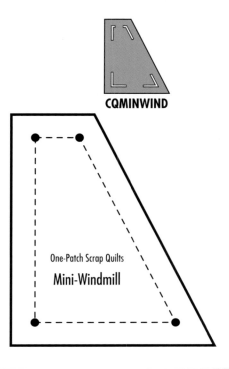

CQMINWIND

One-Patch Scrap Quilts

Mini-Windmill

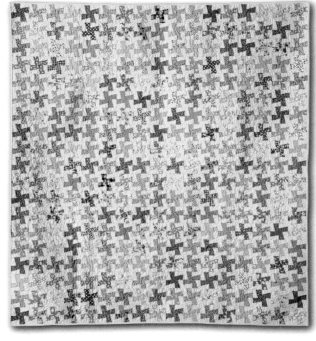

m MEDIUM Slanted Triangle

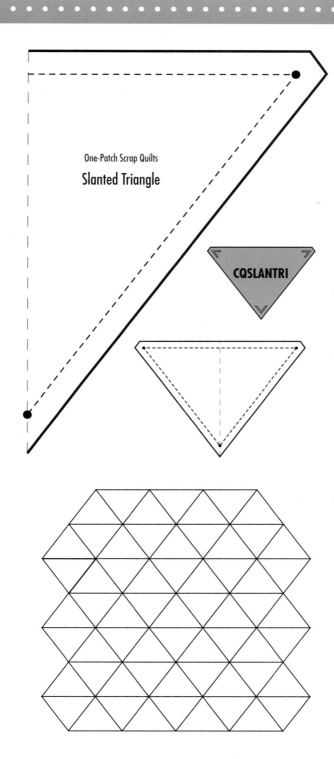

One-Patch Scrap Quilts
Slanted Triangle

CQSLANTRI

SLANTED TRIANGLE, 36½" x 39½", made by Susan Head, Chula Vista, California. Using your batik scraps with one neutral color makes an effective One-Patch design. Why not try something different by using a narrow flange inner border? It's a great finishing touch.

MEDIUM

Half-Square Triangle

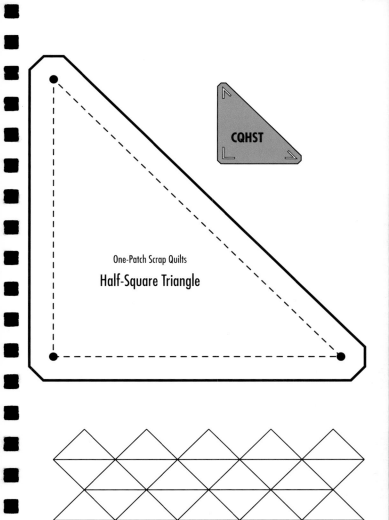

CQHST

One-Patch Scrap Quilts

Half-Square Triangle

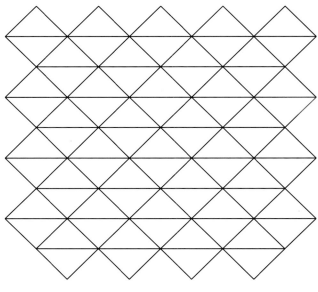

HALF-SQUARE TRIANGLE, 39" x 39", made by Peggy Weichel, Mt. Plymouth, Florida. Using one strong color of your scraps, blended with neutrals of creams and whites, allows the design to float across the background. The swirls in the border fabric set off the straight lines of the triangles.

m MEDIUM

Kite

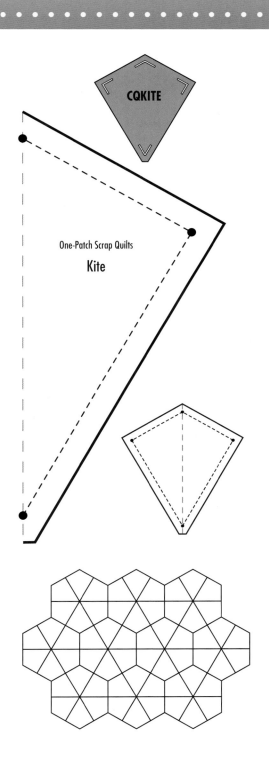

CQKITE

One-Patch Scrap Quilts

Kite

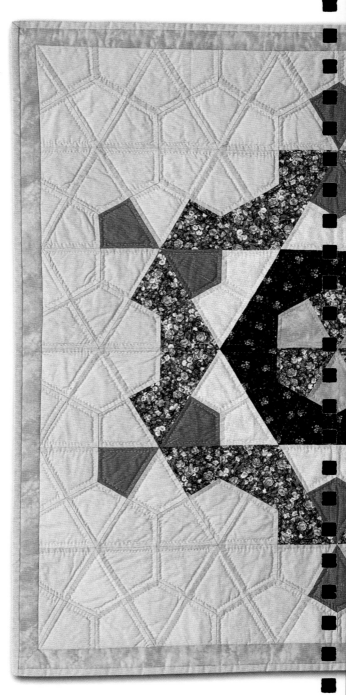

KITE, 37" x 38", made by Carol Louise Michaud, Holtsville, New York. Look at the design possibilities when putting a traditional hexagon block setting in the middle and continuing with a more contemporary placement of the kite pieces. Hand quilting outlines the shapes and adds interest to the quilt.

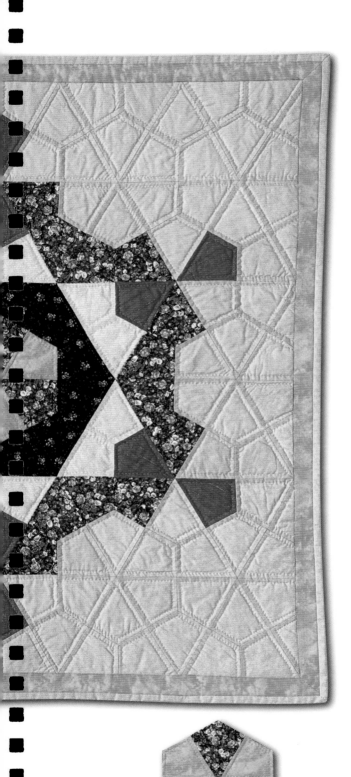

Hexagon

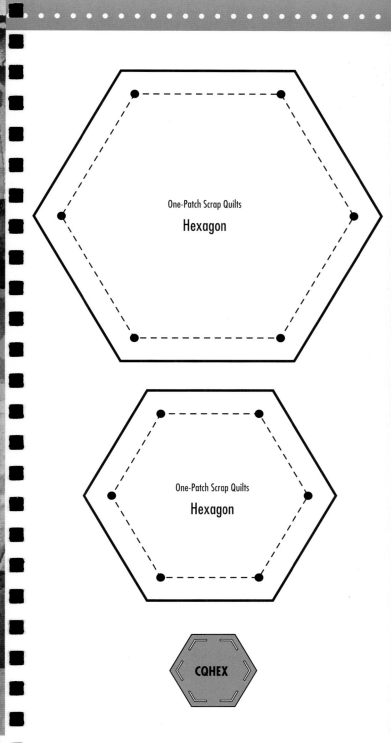

One-Patch Scrap Quilts

Hexagon

One-Patch Scrap Quilts

Hexagon

CQHEX

HEXAGON, 16" x 20", made by the author. Incorporating one of the most popular shapes used in quilts for more than a century, this quilt is not your ordinary Grandmother's Flower Garden, but an exercise in using batik scraps. Ninety-nine percent of quilters have made at least one quilt using this shape and no two quilts are ever alike.

m MEDIUM Half Hexagon

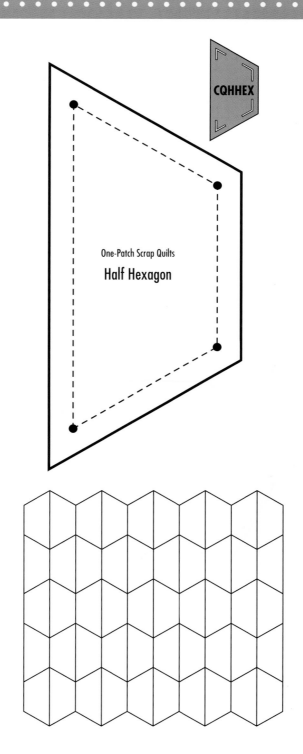

CQHHEX

One-Patch Scrap Quilts

Half Hexagon

HALF HEXAGON, 39½" x 36½", made by Susie
Anderson and quilted by Margaret Phillips, both of
Cos Cob, Connecticut. Many colorful scraps from the
color wheel were used to create this half-hexagon quilt.
Fanciful quilting of flowers and tulip buds help to
create the garden-like appeal. Just take care to match
the seams before you sew them!

MEDIUM **Half Hexagon**

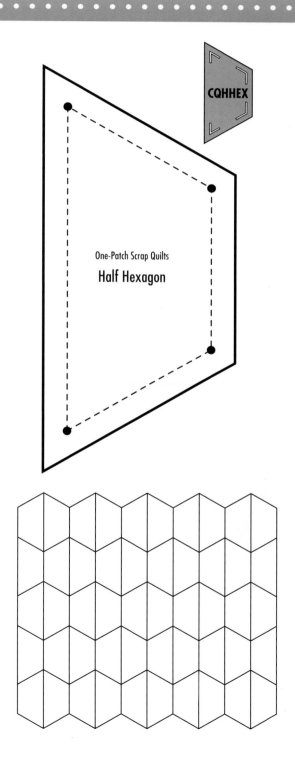

CQHHEX

One-Patch Scrap Quilts

Half Hexagon

HALF HEXAGON, 39½" x 36½", made by Susie Anderson and quilted by Margaret Phillips, both of Cos Cob, Connecticut. Many colorful scraps from the color wheel were used to create this half-hexagon quilt. Fanciful quilting of flowers and tulip buds help to create the garden-like appeal. Just take care to match the seams before you sew them!

*M*EDIUM **Twisted Tumbler**

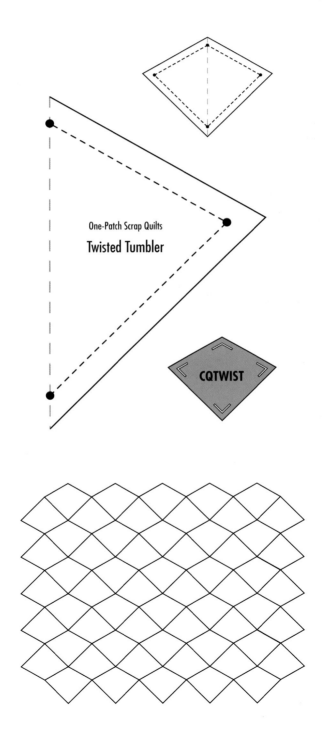

One-Patch Scrap Quilts
Twisted Tumbler

CQTWIST

TWISTED TUMBLER, 46½" x 46½", made by
Margrette Carr, San Diego, California. A take-off on
the popular Tumbler template adds an entirely different look and is a great choice for a charm quilt.
Machine quilting with variegated thread, stitched from
point to point of the pattern shapes, enhances the
overall look of the quilt.

m MEDIUM **Pentagon**

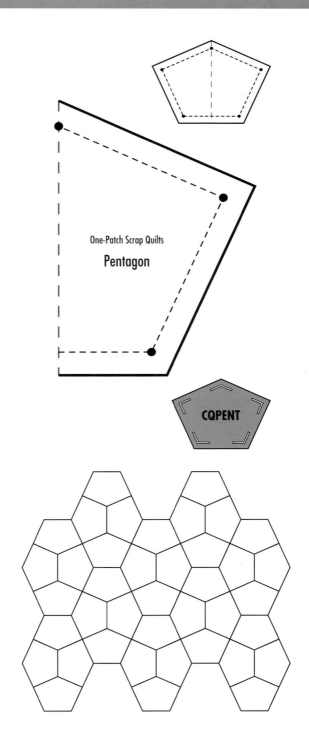

One-Patch Scrap Quilts
Pentagon

CQPENT

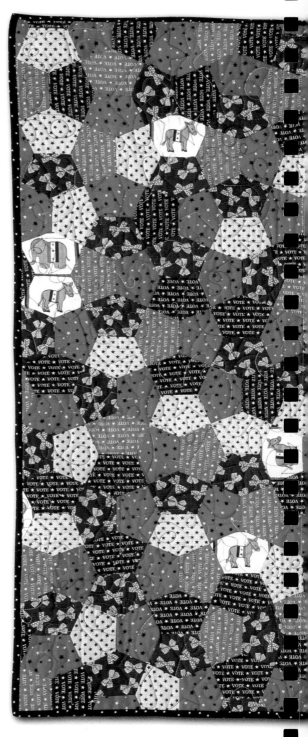

PENTAGON, 30½" x 38½", made by the author. Using a bundle of coordinated political fabric makes this a great conversation piece. Machine quilting was done in meandering lines and stars, keeping with the theme of the fabric. Choose your own theme and have fun finding the right fabrics.

m MEDIUM **Baby Rattle**

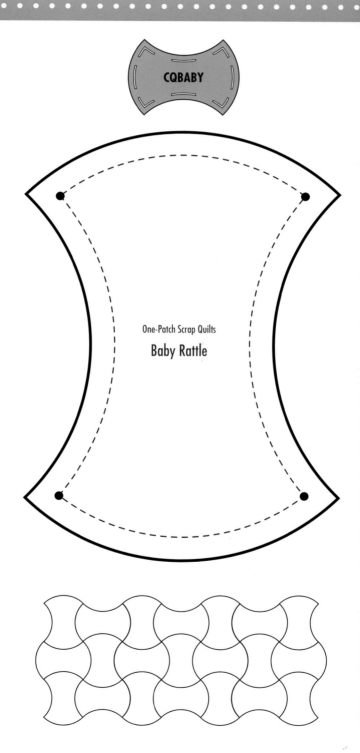

CQBABY

One-Patch Scrap Quilts

Baby Rattle

BABY RATTLE (FRIENDSHIP CURVE),
42" x 42", made by Diane Weber, Cupertino,
California. The gentle curve is simple to sew, allowing
your seams to lie flat. Once again, choosing to use a
color-coordinated collection works well in the overall
design pattern. Choosing a striped fabric to bind
the edges of the pattern makes the quilt even more
interesting.

m MEDIUM   **Baby Block**

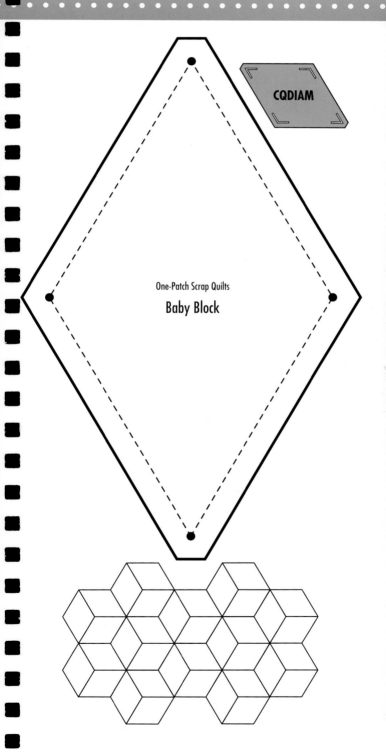

CQDIAM

One-Patch Scrap Quilts
Baby Block

BABY BLOCK (60-DEGREE DIAMONDS),
25½" x 35", made by the author. The placement of
fabric in this quilt allows you to easily pick out the patterns (Stars and Baby Blocks). Bright colors pulsate,

keeping the shapes constantly moving. The meandering quilting stitches with multicolored thread
enhance the overall design.

House

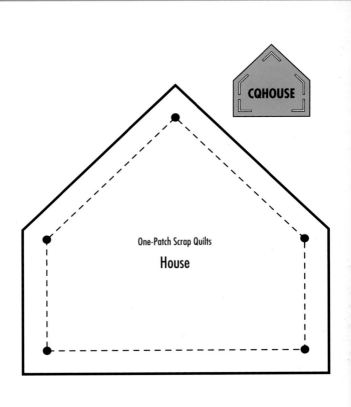

CQHOUSE

One-Patch Scrap Quilts

House

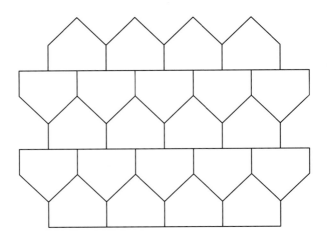

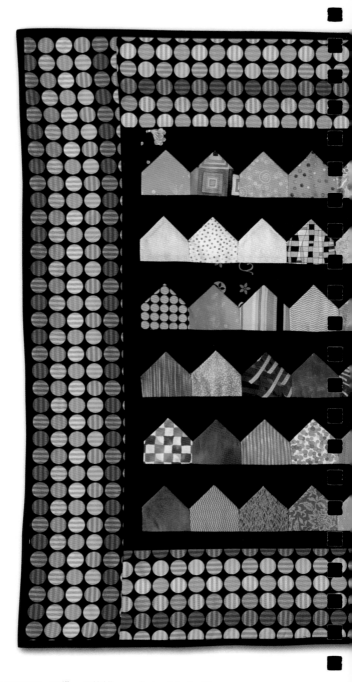

HOUSE, 36" x 34½", made by Linda Denner,
Warrensburg, New York. A fun pattern to work
with — creating houses from Benjamin Moore®
paint colors and a polka dot print. Try your hand at
building a neighborhood in your choice of colors!

HARDER

Elongated Pentagon

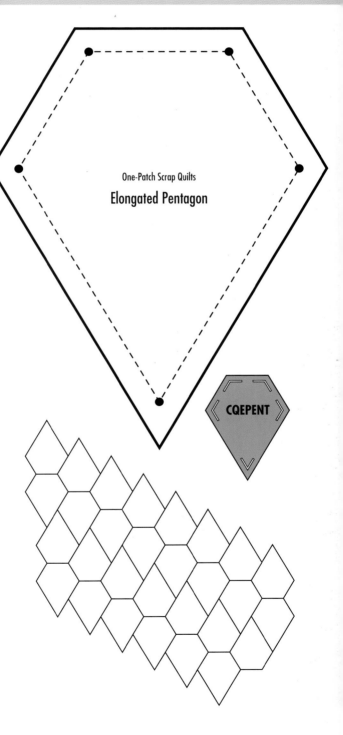

One-Patch Scrap Quilts

Elongated Pentagon

CQEPENT

ELONGATED PENTAGON, 30" x 31", made
by Marge Geary, Williston Park, New York. Using your
batik scraps can result in this "waterfall" look. Use your
imagination and the schematic drawing on page 79 to
see how many setting variations you can come up with.
Easy diagonal machine quilting completes the look.

HARDER

Bottle

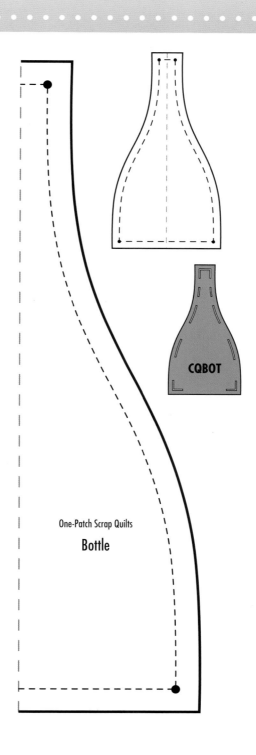

CQBOT

One-Patch Scrap Quilts
Bottle

BOTTLE, 42½" x 43½", made by Michele Miroff, Huntington, New York. An interesting nesting pattern works well in this color arrangement. Why not try using prints with objects found in bottles as another idea? Use your imagination to create you own version. Interconnecting circles were hand quilted on this piece. (Bets Ramsey has graciously given me permission to use this block.)

HARDER

Honeycomb

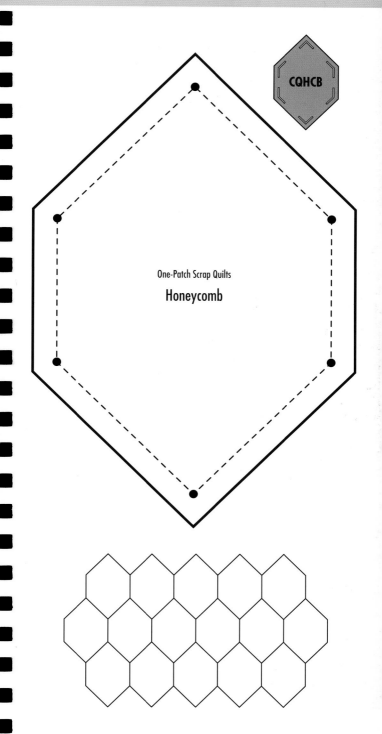

CQHCB

One-Patch Scrap Quilts

Honeycomb

HONEYCOMB, 28½" x 38", made by Margrette Carr, San Diego, California. A favorite One-Patch pattern of mine since it's larger than a hexagon. Many antique quilts have been made using this shape and it's always a "wow!" when I see one. Vertical machine quilting completes this project.

HARDER

Long Honeycomb

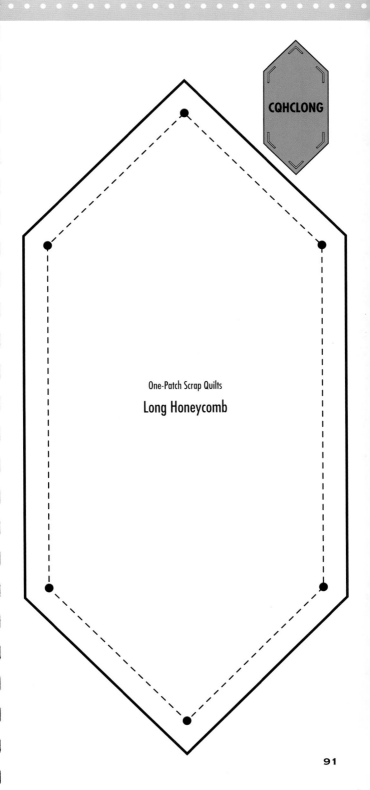

CQHCLONG

One-Patch Scrap Quilts

Long Honeycomb

LONG HONEYCOMB (ELONGATED HEXAGON), 36½" x 45½", made by Nancy Straub, Ephrata, Pennsylvania. Using a color-coordinated bundle of fabrics allows you to create a pleasing palette without much searching for just the right fabrics for your project. Hand quilting splits the hexagon in two directions and gives added dimension. Using a dark inner border contains the design.

H ARDER **Parallelogram**

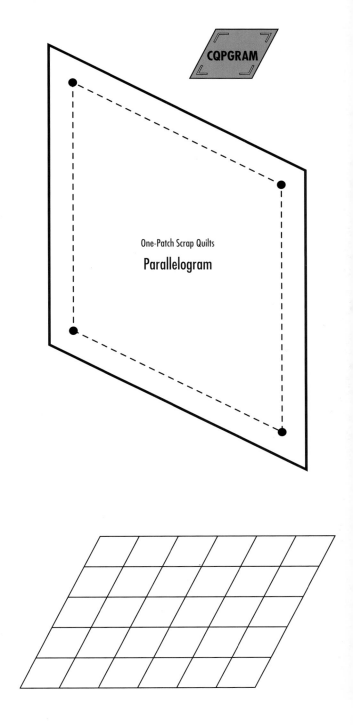

CQPGRAM

One-Patch Scrap Quilts

Parallelogram

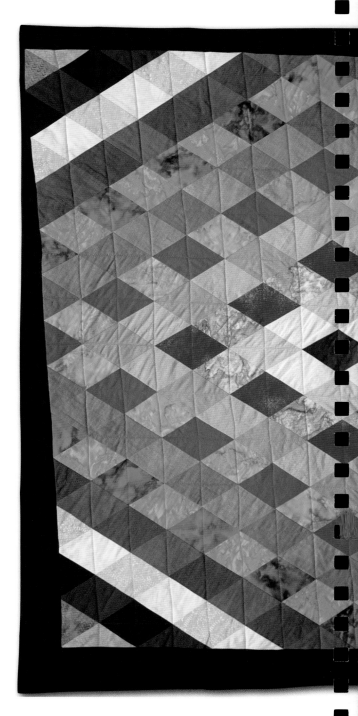

PARALLELOGRAM, 39¾" x 39¾", made by
Linda Salitrynski, Rome, Pennsylvania. This pattern will
stretch your creativity to use fabrics and designs to push
you "out of the box." The varied colors of grey create their
own diamond pattern within the parallelogram. A design
wall is very helpful when working with this template.

H HARDER **3-D Hexagon**

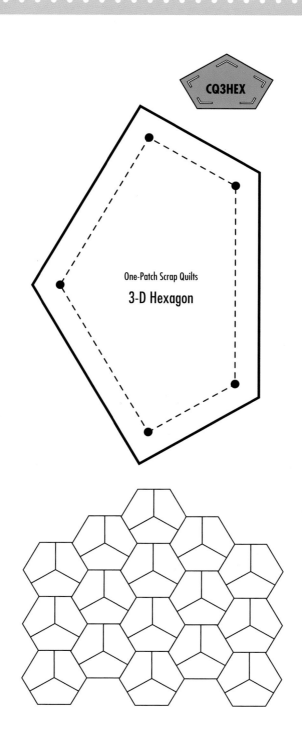

CQ3HEX

One-Patch Scrap Quilts
3-D Hexagon

3-D HEXAGON, 32" x 36", made by Linda Gresham, Mt. Dora, Florida. Using light, medium, and dark scraps to piece together this 3-D hexagon creates a whimsical look. Machine stitching in the ditch works well as it does not distract from the overall design. Clever use of striped binding fabric ties it all together.

H HARDER   **Coffin**

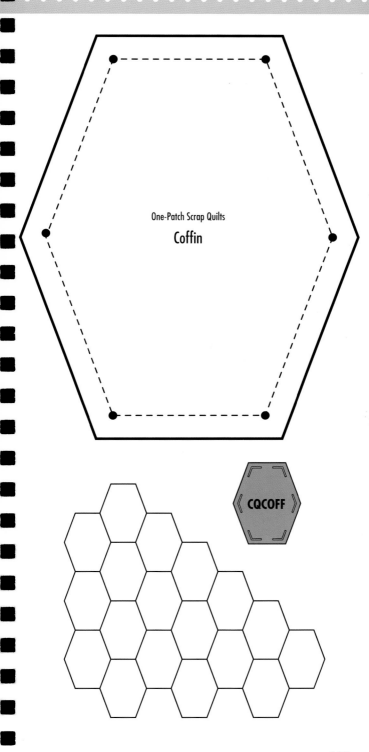

One-Patch Scrap Quilts

Coffin

CQCOFF

COFFIN, 38¾" x 38½", made by Linda Salitrynski, Rome, Pennsylvania. The jewel tones of this quilt give it a happy, upbeat feeling. In earlier days this pattern was used to cover a coffin and afterwards given to the family of the deceased. The color choices would have been very somber back then.

BRAID, 27½" x 30½", made by Linda Denner, Warrensburg, New York. This is a perfect template to use for a vertical stripping quilt. The braided piece can face in either direction. A flowering vine was quilted between the strips. Turn to page 108 for a different setting possibility using this shape.

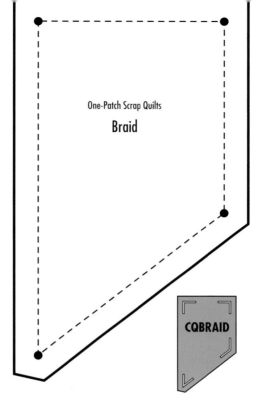

One-Patch Scrap Quilts
Braid

CQBRAID

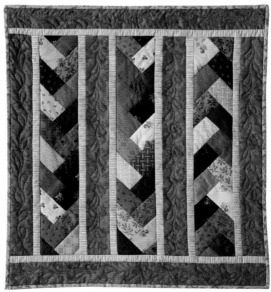

PICKET FENCE, 33" x 24¾", made by
Margrette Carr, San Diego, California. This is the
same shaped template as the Braid, pages 106–107,
but uses a different grainline and angle placement.
Bright colored fabric was used to create zigzag rows
and all quilting was done in the ditch.

HARDER **Picket Fence**

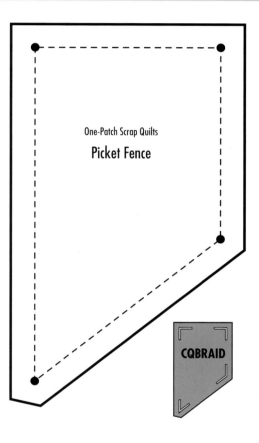

One-Patch Scrap Quilts

Picket Fence

CQBRAID

*H*ARDER Cracker

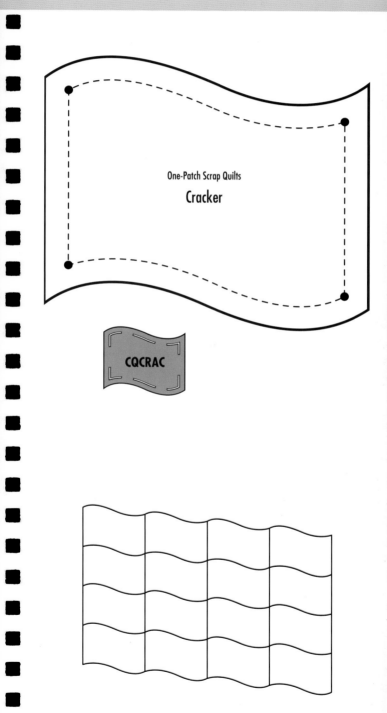

One-Patch Scrap Quilts
Cracker

CQCRAC

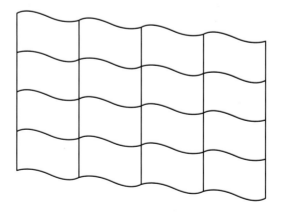

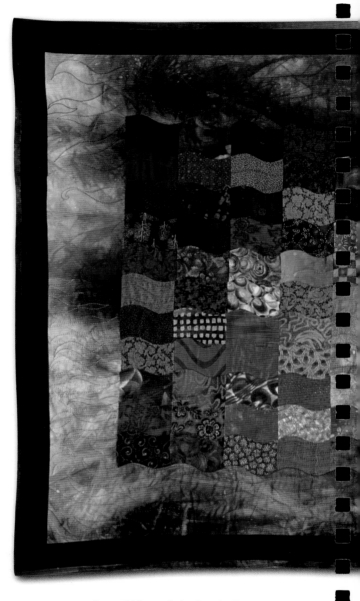

CRACKER, 39" x 32½", made by Linda Denner, Warrensburg, New York. A modern version of a very old pattern is shown here in jewel batiks combined with scraps. The hand-dyed border sets off the design and a wavy machine-quilting pattern adds movement to the quilt.

HARDER **Spinning Star**

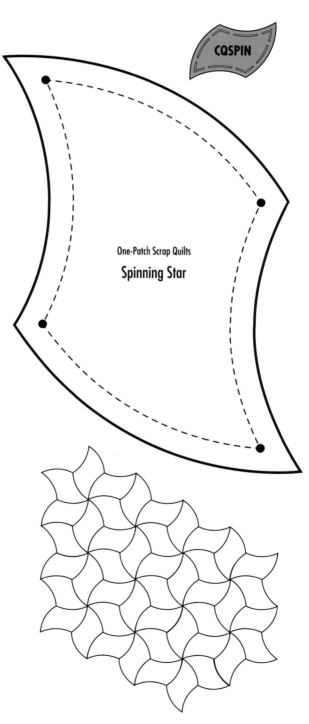

CQSPIN

One-Patch Scrap Quilts
Spinning Star

SPINNING STAR, 46" x 44½", made by Mary Shurpik, Stonybrook, New York. What a great challenge working with curves to create spinning stars! The colors pulsate creating a visual dance. The well chosen border fabric continues the movement and the various freehand filler patterns highlight the six-pointed stars.

HARDER

Clamshell

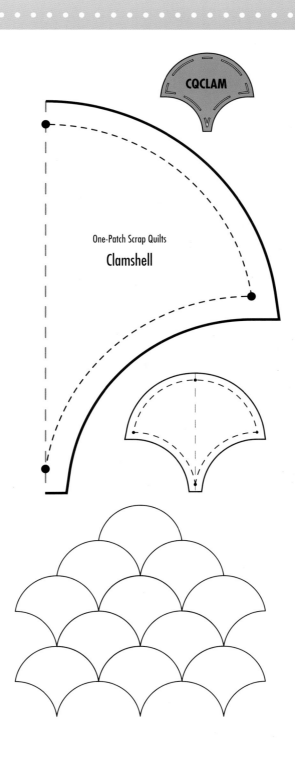

CQCLAM

One-Patch Scrap Quilts
Clamshell

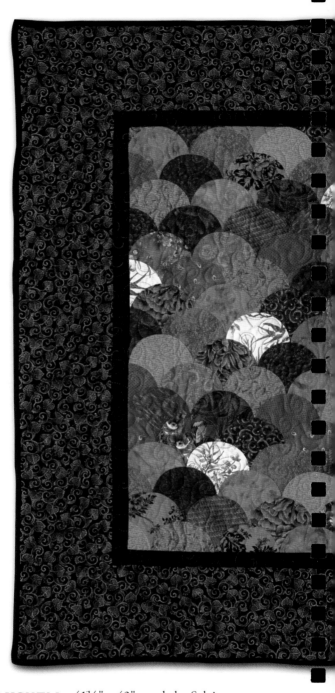

CLAMSHELL, 41½" x 43", made by Sylvia
Frontz, San Diego, California. The fabulous array of
red fabrics creates a warm feeling for this design. Why
not choose from your favorite color palette to sew
your own clamshell quilt? The wide border works well
showcasing this quilt.

H HARDER   Quilter's Fan

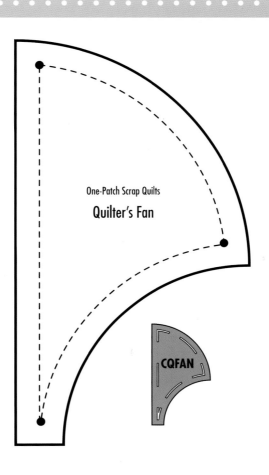

One-Patch Scrap Quilts
Quilter's Fan

CQFAN

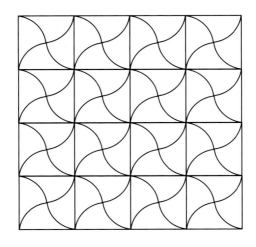

QUILTER'S FAN, 39" x 39", made by Dee Danley Brown, Magalia, California. This is a *Kansas City Star* pattern that stretches your sewing skill to create a scrappy quilt. A clever use of light and dark batiks creates a look of continual motion. Consider strip-piecing leftover fabric to create an interesting binding.

*B*BONUS   **Marble**

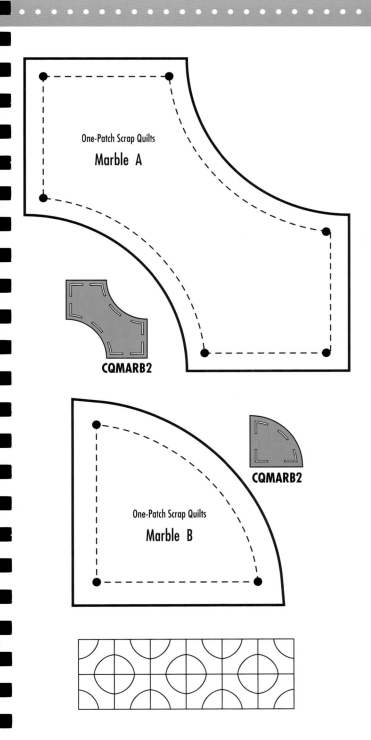

One-Patch Scrap Quilts
Marble A

CQMARB2

CQMARB2

One-Patch Scrap Quilts
Marble B

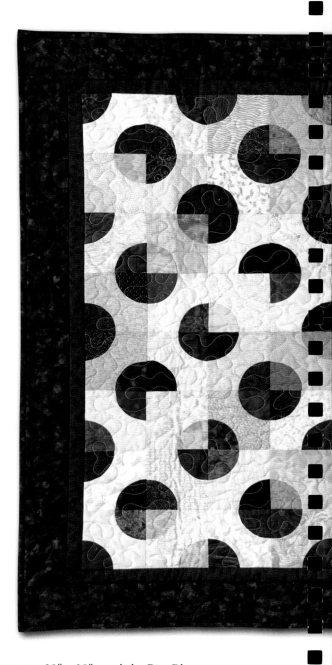

MARBLE, 39" x 38", made by Rita Rhem
and quilted by Sandra Frizzell, both of Hebron,
Connecticut. This pattern is also from the *Kansas City
Star* collection and was a very popular choice to showcase light and dark fabrics. The corner quarter circles
feature medium and dark fabrics and the background
uses lights. By reversing the colors you can give this
bonus pattern a completely different look.

Ozark Tile

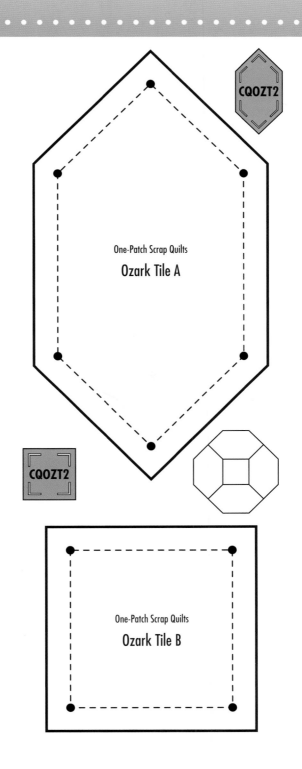

One-Patch Scrap Quilts
Ozark Tile A

CQOZT2

CQOZT2

One-Patch Scrap Quilts
Ozark Tile B

OZARK TILE, 35½" x 36½", made by Judy Klein, Queens, New York. This bonus pattern works well with scraps. The center squares could be used for signature blocks or to form a secondary pattern. The idea is to be able to showcase the scrappy fabric, using a muslin or solid background. The idea came from the late 1930s when quilters wanted to start organizing their fabric much like we do today.

B BONUS

Ozark Cobblestone

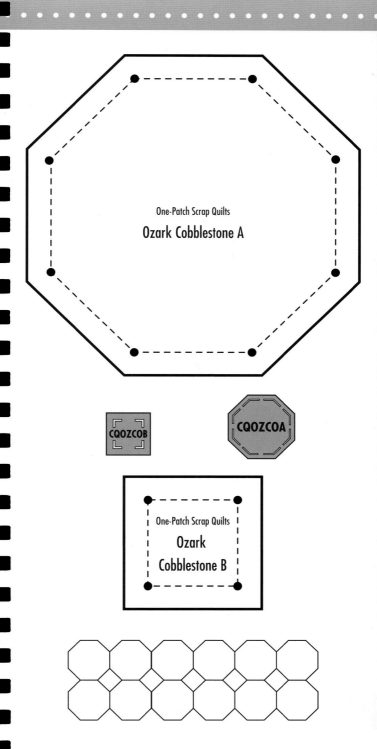

One-Patch Scrap Quilts

Ozark Cobblestone A

CQOZCOB

CQOZCOA

One-Patch Scrap Quilts

Ozark Cobblestone B

OZARK COBBLESTONE, 38" x 38", made by Madalene Becker, Denver, Colorado. Another bonus pattern using two pieces, but still counted as a One-Patch design that showcases your collection of scraps using a neutral square. The fabric selection could be reversed and the center octagons could be in the neutral color, perfect for fancy quilting motifs.

B BONUS   Ice Cream Cone

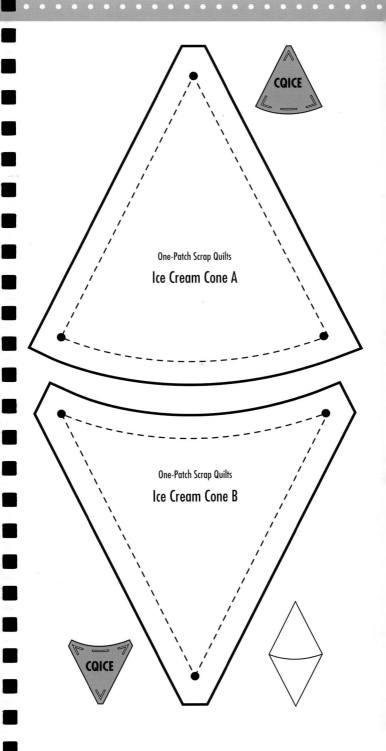

One-Patch Scrap Quilts
Ice Cream Cone A

One-Patch Scrap Quilts
Ice Cream Cone B

CQICE

CQICE

ICE CREAM CONE, 35" x 36", made by
Margrette Carr, San Diego, California. A very old
pattern from the mid-1800s makes this quilt a treasure
and a wonderful showcase for your scrap collection. It
also makes a great charm quilt, with every fabric being
different.

Resources

These templates can be purchased at local quilt shops, fabric stores, mail-order supply companies, or order directly from:
www.Comequiltwithme.com

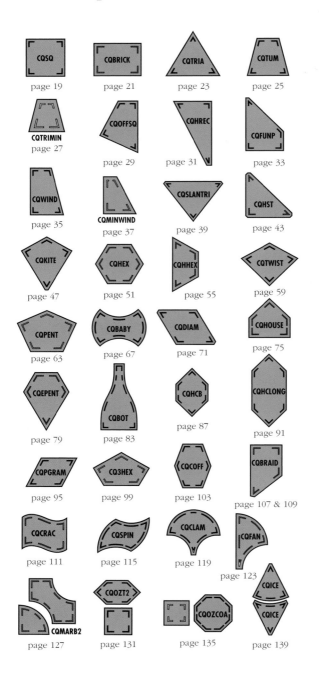

CQSQ
page 19

CQBRICK
page 21

CQTRIA
page 23

CQTUM
page 25

CQTRIMIN
page 27

CQOFFSQ
page 29

CQHREC
page 31

CQFUNP
page 33

CQWIND
page 35

CQMINWIND
page 37

CQSLANTRI
page 39

CQHST
page 43

CQKITE
page 47

CQHEX
page 51

CQHHEX
page 55

CQTWIST
page 59

CQPENT
page 63

CQBABY
page 67

CQDIAM
page 71

CQHOUSE
page 75

CQEPENT
page 79

CQBOT
page 83

CQHCB
page 87

CQHCLONG
page 91

CQPGRAM
page 95

CQ3HEX
page 99

CQCOFF
page 103

CQBRAID
page 107 & 109

CQCRAC
page 111

CQSPIN
page 115

CQCLAM
page 119

CQFAN
page 123

CQMARB2
page 127

CQOZT2
page 131

CQOZCOA
page 135

CQICE
CQICE
page 139

About the Author

Pat Yamin has been quilting for over 30 years. She has amassed a large collection of antique quilt tops and blocks. Her collections are frequently requested for trunk shows and have been invited for exhibition at a number of major shows across the country.

A pioneer in the quilting field, she started Come Quilt With Me in 1981. It has evolved from a mail-order company to become a major manufacturing concern. Her antique quilts serve as design inspiration for the acrylic templates her company manufactures. Pat is also the inventor of the Brooklyn Revolver™, an assortment of rotary-cutting turntables popular with quilters the world over.

Pat has appeared on numerous television programs, most recently the *American Quilter* on Lifetime TV. She has also been a frequent guest on the *Martha Stewart Living* radio show.

From her base in Brooklyn, New York, she travels extensively to national quilting events and is frequently asked to teach, lecture, and judge. Her booth is always packed with customers looking for the newest gadget Pat has either invented or found to sell to quilters.

Another AQS book by the author: *Back to Basics: Quilt Templates & Patterns Explained*

Other AQS Books

This is only a small selection of the books available from the American Quilter's Society. AQS books are known worldwide for timely topics, clear writing, beautiful color photos, and accurate illustrations. The following books are available from your local bookseller, quilt shop, or public library.

#7486   us$19.95

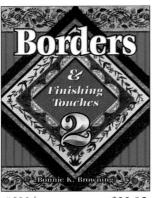

#6804   us$22.95

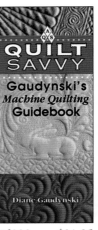

#6898   us$21.95

#6519   us$21.95

#6520   us$21.95

#6413   us$21.95